1

Towards *new Arabic world*

Democracy Of Blood Weddings!

Wrriten in arabic in 2008

Mamdouh Al-Shikh

2

Book title:

Democracy Of Blood Weddings!

Towards new Arabic world

Author: Mamdouh Al-Shikh

ISBN-13: 978-1467915007

ISBN-10: 1467915009

Publisher: The author

Frist print 2011.

4

Democracy Of Blood Weddings!

The "**Blood weddings**" expression has come to be the only one that is able to summarize the political scene of the Arab world, as well as some bordering regions which constitute the Islamic depth of the Arab world. In the conflict on Palestine, the Palestinian blood bridals are almost continuous. Although this might be understood in the conflict with **"the Other"**, and within the framework of relations with the foreign world, what is surprising and frightening is that this might be a summary of the internal clashes.

In the period between the assassinations of Banazeer Butu, Pakistani former Prime Minister, and Rafiq El-Hariri, the Lebanese Prime Minister, there have been a long queue of blood wedding, whose purpose is not the liberation of the national land but the confiscation of the future of both the nation and the citizen.

Reflecting this gloomy scene, I feel afraid of the

kinds of fruits that fall down upon us from this tree of national liberation, which we have planted with our own hands, in the hope of plucking there from the most delicious fruits. It is true that the change for better was the call of all of those movements (of liberation), how then have we gone downhill as such?

In order to answer (this question), one needs to be patient to quietly deal with the concepts, and not simply (to repeat) the slogans. Verily, the change for better is a complex process, in which political, cultural and social considerations are interrelated to form an equation, whose premises should lead to conclusions.

Since the Arabs took on their trip of economic and social construction, in the wake of the departure of military colonization, such terms as **"development"**, **"growth"** and **"progress"** have come to run on the mouth of the academics and politicians in their sermons and lectures, if not all the learned audience (in their general speech).

Of course, the different international contexts, after independence, played a great role to drive most of those (countries) to adopt the socialist model. Because of the conflict on Palestine, the values of some Arab military institutions rose, in what seemed at the time to be natural reaction to face the challenge imposed by the long military arm. However, there was interaction between military nature and socialist nature, which came to be the main colour, unique to most Arab economies, which had a great impact not only on the culture, but also on the structure of society in general.

With the Socialist option, the change led by the highest elite became dominant, which, in turn, relegated to the margin the role of individual initiatives. In this way, the concept of the sudden drastic change and the way of collective mobilization, with its different forms became prevalent, in order to have control over the path of economic developments, and all of its factors. Thus, Socialism brought forth its literature and culture.

Moreover, some became so much ambitious that they had a dream of building a "**Revolutionary Socialist human**". This was a result of a process of wide-ranging control over the factors of social change. The society did not create its own culture, policy and economic pattern, but ideology, instead, replaced man, and it further brutalized in its dream of building its own human.

Certainly, the autocratic Marxist and nationalist ideologies have not solved the problem of poverty, as their slogans claimed: on the contrary, they acted as factories of destitution. Therefore, with the lack of good learning, and the absence of peacefully sheer taking of power by turns, the atmosphere was appropriate for giving sanctity to the collective tendencies, which turned to be an established situation, and human character. It is from this point in particular, that the idea of having an aversion to Capitalism, and ascribing to it the most odious attributes, and considering it to be a Western conspiracy to pauperize peoples was born. However, it was an unjustifiably collective situation.

Until now, we have not yet been able to assimilate the fact that Socialism is not the most appropriate way of development, a fact understood by many countries which turned to market economies within a limited number of years after long decades of Communism, without giving sanctity to any economic system as a national choice. It has been affirmed, by virtue of the collapse of Berlin Wall, that Capitalism is able to ensure an endurable framework of developing and managing a modern economy. But it is accused, in our world, of saving luxury only for a very few in a great ocean of human misery.

To be sure, the relation of policy with economy could, by no means, be restricted to the fair distribution of returns; but it includes the process of evolution development. In the middle of policy, there is the answer to the most important question of economic evolution, i.e. the relation the culture has with the authority, and the role it plays in the evolution. The cultural dimension creates values, rules, symbols, and governing conventions of practicing authority. The public's yearning for a **"charismatic"** leader stems from some myths which give legitimacy to the individual authority. But even, such leadership hinders the development of the institutional state. This continues to remain in our countries, although there are evidences for the early awareness of the great danger of the individual leader. **"The individual men are unable to ensure the future (of nations)"** as Napoleon Bonaparte stated in the beginning of the nineteenth century, **"For it is the institutions alone which determine the fate of nations."**

With the rise of the "**charismatic**" leader, the specialized economists disappear, leaving the arena to the apologists and eulogists, and those who raise slogans which are more general and emotional than scientific and responsive to logic and reasoning. Being so, some economic activities are consecrated only for their being indicative to the national identity. Thus, change seems as though being treacherous to the forefathers. Certainly, it is incumbent upon us to respect our forefathers, but, without ruining the future of our grandchildren.

More often, overindulgence is concomitant to the rise of a

"**charismatic**" leader. As far as our instance is concerned, the elite of national liberation have failed to distinguish between a "**cruel state**" and a "**powerful state**". A "**violent state**" could hardly be a "**powerful state**", because it mainly depends upon compulsive and administrative ways to break in the society, whereas the "**powerful state**" uses both leniency and persuasion, therewith its capability of change for better becomes obvious, through co-operation with, and not by having dominance over the centres of forces in the society.

Therefore, the autocracy, which does not abide by any

legal restrictions allows for the state to be arbitrary in its behaviours, and gives a false impression of its absolute power. But very soon, this false impression vanishes with the emergence of loopholes of application. This state uses both symbolism and allegory to support its ruling. But it seldom endeavours to achieve legitimacy through good performance. The ability of a certain state to collect direct, instead of indirect taxes provides a reliable indicator of its actual power on the one hand, and of the people's acceptance of its legitimacy on account of its good performance on the other hand. However, the claims of autocracy to hasten the process of development should not be considered only for its apparent value.

There is in the minds of most decision makers, and many of our cultured men, an idea, in which there is no distinction between "**power**" and "**force**". The power is to have unlimited force, as well as to have compelling influence, which summons ideal behaviours for which it receives admiration and submission. It is undoubtedly associated with authority, but not necessarily with force, which is to coerce others to do what they would have not done, had it not been for compulsion.

It is of great importance to distinguish between power and force, since it admits the fact that the state could hardly have inexhaustible stock of force upon which it persistently relies; but rather, the coercive force should be used moderately, and it instead should fundamentally depend upon its power to obtain unanimity on its policies, in order to ensure a voluntary response.

The concept of the "**powerful state**" referred to (as violent) has become out of date. With the world increasing interest in the human rights and civil society, the internal power of a state could not be measured by its suppressive force so much as by its capability of crystallizing a collective consensus which puts freedom on the same level with security. One of the most dangerous results of the preconception of the choice of having **"dominance"** over society is to policize the role of security bodies. To summon the security forces to the political arena leads not only to the turning of political act from debate and competition to clashes but also it has, at the same time, a more dangerous result, i.e. those bodies turn to be decision makers. At this point, both bullet and truncheon become dominant; and with enlarging their authority, those bodies almost always turn to be a **"political party"**, and as the security bodies enter the political arena from the door, democracy comes out of "**the window**".

Aspiration, Prophecy And Futuristic Perspective

It might be neither accurate nor factual to talk about the Arab intellect, and make absolute judgements on it. But it is certainly reasonable to admit the fact that a mostly left wing-(Marxist and Nationalist) -controlled intellectual trend has been leading the Arab culture for more than sixty years, namely, since we came out of the pit of autocracy to go down into a pitfall of despotism-might it not be bottomless, let's ask Allah.

This intellect, however, suffers, among many things, from being fascinated by the past in the way it sees its own self and the world as well. When Ibn Khaldun laid the foundations of sociology, he, perhaps unknowingly, laid the foundations of futuristics. The attempt to abstract rules for human construction necessarily required that some of those should almost be firmly constant; and as those laws were attained, expectation and prospect (of future) could be available.

As well as policy is to accommodate opposites and have the opponents enter into negotiations, the political planning of future is an endeavour to control such factors as would interact unreservedly in case of being left with no interference. Here, we could find a bullion of real perception, reckoned imagination and ambition to anticipate what will come to happen.

The future, however, is a broad area of possibilities, which might turn, by virtue of piercing sight, to become a plan which could probably be achieved, no matter great it might seem. To depend on the reality as the beginning and ending limit of political view leads to rigidity and turning from the position of being effective to that of being affected. Although there are, in any universal view, some determinants of the futuristic vision, on which one could rely in building (his own), the Arab political intellect has failed even to imagine.

If one assesses the economic experiments of the East-Asian countries during the second half of the last century, and makes comparison between them and the produce of ours during the same period, he would be astonished by the large gap between our (**capabilities**" and "**value**". For instance, the economic experiments of the Asian Tigers would not have been successful, without a daring political imagination, a quality characteristic of the nations which are rich in their cultures, when they fall victims of the fear that their existence is at risk: thus, every step they think to take becomes questionable and susceptible to reluctance.

Let's take, for example, the collapse of the Soviet Union, which was, for the Americans, an aspiration, a prophecy, and a futuristic perspective. By virtue of this aspiration, they became hopeful, and by virtue of prophecy, they became confident, and the futuristic perspective acted as a bridge between what really was and what was hoped to come.

Along the history of the West, many notions of the

future of the world were raised. It is true that some of them were born and died as no more than notions, but futuristics turned from being merely astrology to a science, which narrowed the gap between talking about, and planning for the future.

When the Arab decision makers have a file, carrying the title: "**As such we want the world to be**", we shall have begun our way to build the future, not through hopes and building high walls to protect us from the futuristic scenarios of others, but by having a ceiling that is fitting for the ambitions of a nation, which has such of capabilities as to enable it to contribute in forming the future of the world. To be sure, the future, which we make no effort to imagine and plan, is mostly mysterious which would, inevitably, destroy us, while we are heedless. To think in the present, and plan for the future are inseparable. How many a present that devastated or even buried the future before it came into existence.

Nevertheless, the lack of balance leads to contradiction between the ethics of the hope and the wholehearted elegies on our state. The ethics of hope are exceedingly flourishing in our culture, and no less thriving are the bitter elegies on our state; and between both contradictory extremes, there is lack of ideas, although the last two centuries were the golden age of ideas, with their important role in history, to the extent that the ideas pushed away, evermore, the role of such factors as power, will, natural resources, and population weight in determining the form of the future.

What is intended by the absence of ideas is the lack of the great ideas, which are the engines of history. Both Capitalism and Socialism, the great ideas of the nineteenth and twentieth centuries, were born in the West. The same is true of the great ideas of administration, international law and technological organization. Moreover, there were no important ideas in our culture of the military thought. In spite of the emerging rise of the military spirit in our countries, we had no single thinker to be included in the row of the makers of the history of military thought, among such names as the Chinese Son Tzu, the German Calusfitz, etc.

One reason for the lack of great ideas in our world is the intentional relegation of the thought makers. In Japan, under the Fascist ruling, the politicians and thinkers were enemies. The politicians were given authority, with its benefits, although they had the lowest levels of culture. On the other hand, the aversion which the thinkers had towards the politicians, besides their lack of financial independence, caused them to be prevented from political participation. In this way, their role remained limited; and they were so much weak that they were given such names as the "**Weak Thinkers**", the "**disgraced Flatterers**". For this reason, they were not able to curb the uncontrollable aspirations of the Japanese men of war, which led Japan to devastation.

Another reason for the absence of the great ideas is the lack of differentiation between values and ideas. The values and standards set by Islam in the human society led some to think that using them only was sufficient for evolution. The result was that most cultured men did not engage themselves in the matter of ideas. Undoubtedly, those values were appreciated, when Umar Ibn Al-Khattab, for instance, applied the idea of registries, the idea which was considered to be a turning point in history. The solution then introduced by Islam was in the field of standards and objectives, and not of means and ways.

Moving to the Arab reality, we shall find that didactic

institutions have turned to be "**high schools**" which bring about thousands of graduates, who are lacking the quality of effective creative personality, and critical thinking. This sin is caused by our certain belief that all solutions have been predetermined, and all we have to do is to work, and then the advancement will ensue without human intervention

With the absence of the factual circumstances under which the ideas might play their role in the reality, the factories of ideas have disappeared, in an attempt to neutralize and trim the nails of the civil society in entirety, including its political parties, associations, and endowments, in a general atmosphere which was prevalent in our country with the rise of the national state. Now, nearly fifty years after (World War II), those who came out of the overwhelming destruction of World War II won the competition with those nations who were released, at the same time, from the grip of colonization. However, the winners were armed with great ideas, whereas the losers were armed only with will.

Therefore, the problem is much deeper than to make comparison between the raised ideas and the relative weights of their followers, or even the validity of their argument. The Arab citizen has the impression that it is a problem of usage: What is the significance of evaluating the raised ideas in order to choose one to patronize, unless this choice leads to give the choosers the right to support and call for their adopted ideas, and their competitors to do the same with their own, within the limits of a certain arena, and in accordance with stipulated laws to be respected by all?

How should we envisage that our nation would develop, while its people are deprived of their rights of democracy including the taking of power by turns, and the independent fair judiciary, to balance the relations of all normal and nominal persons, and of economic freedom, to create sheer economic atmosphere of competition, and the right of recognition and inquiry, all in an integrated network of laws and practices, which enable the individual to get information, and have the right to inquire the governor, and watch over the performance of the government?

Verily, to refrain from participating in the present, and cease to dream of better future could hardly be considered as success of the bodies of political security to achieve stability: on the contrary, it is no more than an alarm bell. However, societies are always afflicted by political failure before they burst or die.

The Illusion Of Conflict Between Nationalism And Democracy

It is not pessimistic to say that we came out of the conflict of powers in the twentieth century with our powers destroyed, since the concept of power prevalent among the Arabs does not go beyond the military force. Paradoxically, this has not even ensured for the Arabs their security, which is under the siege of many threats. But we came out of the golden age of ideas with a deep-rooted false impression, which came to be a distinctive feature, i.e. that our countries are suffering from conflict between nationalism and democracy. The ideas which have run on the tongues and pens of many cultured men for decades remained merely arguments, which were not put to test in real battlefields, to help them crystallized.

For this reason, it is not surprising that there is no Arab Socialism or Arab Liberalism, since their existence among the elite is no more than interpretation of Western ideas, as though they are masterpieces of an open museum of thought.

Under such umbrella, there is no clear difference between identity, ideology and policy. The identity is a result of a long interactions between (religious, cultural, social, economic and linguistic) factors; and it is changeable, and open to turning shifts, and it fundamentally deals with cultural problems. Ideology stands almost on the opposite extreme of policy, which is negotiations (between opponents) and accommodation (of the opposites), things unacceptable to ideology, which starts from having the decisive and final word, a point with which policy comes to end.

Returning back a bit, nearly as far as two centuries, the question of evolution has been an Arab concern, and the Arab cultured men have not ceased to do their best efforts to determine its possible contexts. After two centuries, we still continue to study the problems, whereas the evolution experiments in the East and West have been unremitting, in societies, which have not the same material and spiritual capabilities as we have, and even the suffering of some of them from external factors were many times ours.

Whoever considers the prescriptions suggested for remedy, could find black lists of what should be destroyed, and there is no place for that which should be built. There are calls for facing colonization, making use of the capital, and putting an end to reactionism, as though evolution would inevitably be achieved once we do so, for no reason but that evolution is the Arab's fate doomed to come inescapably, which nothing hinders other than those obstacles.

Since there is almost no integrated hypothesis of an Arab project of evolution, our aborted attempts always are evaluated only in the light of the role of the external factors and competence of implementation. But there is no evaluation for the fundaments of the vision. Furthermore, the necessary relation between Arabism and Socialism could not be justifiable, as though it has been preordained by fate, although before the Arabist expansion, Capitalism existed and had many inveterate successes; and it is unreasonable to regard it a "**forbidden fruit**" just because of the past of colonization in our countries. The same is also true of the indefensible relation between nationalism and autocracy, which results in the aggressive attitude of nationalism culture towards democracy, putting in mind that before national military coups, there were successful democratic experiments in our countries. Autocracy then was not necessarily imperative.

The issue of international developmental reports has come to be a yearly occasion for us to feel how critical our situation is. But the more important lesson therein goes beyond the numbers and statistics to necessarily admit our failure; and this is a factual condition for us to seek after a new beginning, in which the difference should be made clearly between identity and ideology, according to which the elite should not confiscate the people's rights of freedom of choice and creation, and, at the same time, the others' experiments of political and social organization should not be wasted because of their attitudes towards our undoubtedly just causes.

It is taken for granted that we are suffering from deterioration of economy, education and freedom, let alone a few exceptions, as though our countries are slowly sinking, and turning to enter into a dark destiny. On the other hand, the calls for reform are besieged by suspicions and accusations, and the endeavours of change are bound by ideas and choices which some like to sanctify, in such a way that to give them up is to violate nationalism and abandon identity, despite the fact that they are ultimately choices, which might possibly be left. Whoever does not learn from the lessons of history ignores, in fact, the best and the most distinctive attribute of man, with which Allah has favoured him (over all the creatures), i.e. that he is a "**being who has history**", and subsequently, he is able to learn from the experience of those who came before him. He, who likes to see the evil consequence of moving against the history, should look at us.

It is a well-established fact of human society that between all human beings, no matter different they might be, there is a common thing, i.e. the instinct. But even, the great rise of Arabism surpassed its role of reinforcing the feeling of being different from the other, the colonizer, and went as far as to act as a cocoon which separated us from the world, and the result was that we came to reduce the vision of our relation with the world by a single statement: "**We are something different**."

Although there are many lessons of rebuilding after the destruction caused by wars, some of them are appalling. It is well-known from the Japanese experiment, that by the end of World War II, more than one hundred Japanese cities had turned to ashes. But it was not after three years that the Japanese people rebuilt what had been destroyed by war. Is our state worse than that of Japan after the end of World War II?

The lesson to be learnt from this is that it is easier to rebuild what has been destroyed by war than to reconstruct what has been ruined by despotism. We are, indeed, bound in the heavy fetters of the way of thinking of our elite more than we are besieged by the conspiracies of our enemies. It is not the opportunity nor the resources so much as it is the courage which we are lacking.

Unfortunately, a lot of our cultured men feel afraid of the "**audience**", which sometimes forces them to hide their real mindsets, and rather adopt mass slogans, in order to propitiate the public opinion. Because of that, the Arab intellect increasingly tends to be less analytic in its dealing with causes, and rather takes situations which tickle feelings and draw forth the cries of admiration.

The luxury of analysis is always beyond the capacity of the mass disposition. This is well expressed by the famous ironic story of a physician who is invited to remedy a patient whose case is hopeless, but even, it is his statement of diagnosis that is considered to be the cause of his death. Thus, the physicians of Arab political analysis run away, just as one runs away from a lion, from the mess of being the first to announce the fact. Since the mood of the audience is that of facing and gathering, in which there is no place for accommodation, to talk about any compromise is always viewed as betrayal, treachery and...

When the political speech is bound by the leader, and reduced to silence by virtue of the audience, there will be nothing of significance or advantage for it to say, and all what to do is to reproduce the leader's speech by way of confirmation or repetition. If it is to go back to the past, its return will be selective, to choose only what might serve the predetermined mindsets, as though we are faced by an operation of psychological treatment, which deals with sentiment and its fancies and not with the mind and its facts and way of thinking.

In this atmosphere, those who take hold of the steering wheel of guiding the audience could suffocate the differing opinion, a scene similar to that of Soviet Union before Gorpatshov, when the calls for reform were suffocated. But here, the audience has replaced the central committee of the Communist

Party, and the bodies of political security. In this way, the audience became a heavy burden to be carried by those who have amassed it, and the cultured no more than a "**waiter**" to serve his master with what he likes, after having been a leading pioneer by whom the people would be guided. Woe to a nation led by the audience!

To conclude, the domination of this mixture of thoughts over the Arab intellect stems from the endless waves of "**Blood Wedding**". Unless we put an end to those "**Wedding**", and succeed to disengage nationalism from democracy, we all, be it rulers or ruled, cultured or audience, will be doomed to sink. The only treatment is democracy, whatever bitter it might taste as some would take firm oaths.

54

ديموقراطية أعراس الدم!

أصبحت **"أعراس الدم"** التعبير المجازي الأكثر قدرة على تلخيص المشهد السياسي العربي وبعض التخوم التي تشكل العمق الإسلامي للعالم العربي. ففي الصراع على فلسطين لا تكاد أعراس الدم الفلسطينية تتوقف، وقد يكون هذا مفهوماً في صراع مع **"الآخر"**، وفي إطار العلاقة مـــع

الخارج، لكن الجديد المخيف أن تصبح أعــراس الدم تلخيصا للتدافع الداخلي.

فبين اغتيال بي نظير بوتو رئــيس وزراء باكستان السابق ورفيق الحريــري رئــيس وزراء لبنان السابق، هناك طابور طويل مــن الأعــراس الدموية، لا لأجل "**تحرير التراب الوطني**"، بــل ربما لأجل مصادرة مستقبل الوطن والمواطن معاً!

وعندما أتأمل هذا المشهد الكئيب أشــعر بالرعب من نوع الثمار التي تتساقط علينــا مــن شجرة "**التحرر الوطني**" التي غرســناها بأيــدينا آملين أن نقطف منها أشهى الثمار، وقد كانــت هذه الحركات جميعاً داعية تغيير للأفضل.

فكيف وصلنا هذا المنحدر؟

الإجابة تحتاج صبراً على معالجة هادئــة للمفاهيم لا الشعارات، فالتغيير للأفضل عمليــة

مركبة تتداخل فيها الاعتبارات السياسية والثقافية
والاجتماعية لتشكل معا معادلة تؤدي مقدماتها
لنتائجها. ومنذ بـدأ العـرب مشـوار البنـاء
الاقتصادي والاجتماعي بعد رحيـل الاسـتعمار
العسكري، ومصطلحات: **"التنميــة"** و**"النمـو"**
و**"التقـدم"**، تتـردد في خطـاب الأكـاديميين
والسياسيين، بل عامة المتعلمين بلا انقطاع.

وبطبيعة الحال، لعبت السياقات الدوليــة
عقب الاستقلال دوراً في دفع معظمها لاسـتلهام
النموذج الاشتراكي. وبسـبب الصـراع علـى
فلسطين، ارتفعت أسهم المؤسسات العسـكرية
عربيا، كاستجابة بـدت – آنـذاك – طبيعيـة
لمواجهة ذراع عسكرية طويلة.

وتفاعلت الطبيعة العسكرية لهذه الأنظمة،
مع الطبيعة الاشتراكية التي أصبحت الصبغة الغالبة

على اقتصاديات معظم الدول العربيـــة — تـــأثيراً وتأثراً — فتركت آثاراً كبيرة على الثقافة، بــل على بنية المجتمعات عموماً.

ومع الخيار الاشتراكي، جاء تغليب التغيير من أعلى، وتهميش دور المبادرات الفردية، وغلبة مفهوم التغيير الجذري الفجائي، وأسلوب الحشد، والجماعية بصيغها المختلفة، وصولاً إلى التحكم في مسار التطورات الاقتصادية، وكل ما يمكـــن أن يؤثر فيها. فأفرزت الاشتراكية أدبهـــا وثقافتـــها، ووصل طموح البعض لأن يحلم ببناء **"الإنسـان الاشتراكي الثوري"**، كثمرة لعمليـــة تَحكـــُّم شاملة في عوامل التغيير الاجتماعي.

فبدلاً من أن يبدع المجتمع ثقافته وسياسته ونموذجه الاقتصادي، حلت الأيـــديولوجيا محـــل الإنسان، ثم تغولت فحلمت ببناء **"إنساهما"**.

وعلى وجه القطع، فإن الأيـــديولوجيات الاستبدادية (الماركسية والقومية) لم تعالج مشكلة الفقر كما ادعت شعاراها، بل كانـــت مصـــانع للفقر. وبغياب التعليم الجيد والتـــدول الســـلمي الشفاف للسلطة أصبح المناخ مهيئا لتقديس الميول الجماعية، ثم تحولت إلى موقف لا يناقش و"**فطرة**" إنسانية، ومن هذا الباب دخلت فكــرة كراهيـــة الرأسمالية، ووصفها بأبشع الأوصاف، واعتبارهـــا مؤامرة غربية لإفقار الشعوب، وهـــو موقـــف جماعي جماهيري غير مبرر.

ونحن لم نستطع حتى الآن "**ابتلاع**" حقيقة أن الاشتراكية ليست الوسيلة الأنسب للتنميـــة، وهي حقيقة استوعبتها دول حكمتها الشـــيوعية لعقود، وتحولت لاقتصـــاديات الســـوق خـــلال سنوات محدودة دون تقديس النظام الاقتصـــادي

بوصفه خياراً وطنياً. فانهيار جدار برلين أثبت أن الرأسمالية تؤمن إطاراً قابلاً للاستمرار لتطوير اقتصاد حديث وإدارته، بينما في عالمنا، تتهم بأنها تؤمن الرفاهية لأقلية، وسط بحر هائل من البؤس الإنساني.

وصلة السياسة بالاقتصاد لا تقتصر على عدالة توزيع العوائد، بل تشمل عملية بناء النهضة نفسها. ففي قلب السياسة تقع إجابة أحد أهم أسئلة النهوض الاقتصادي، وهو صلة الثقافة بالسلطة ودورهما في النهوض. فالبعد الثقافي يخلق القيم والقواعد والرموز والأعراف الحاكمة لممارسة السلطة، وتوق الجماهير لقيادة "كاريزمية" نابع من أساطير تمنح مشروعية لسلطة "الفرد"، ومثل هذه القيادة تؤخر تطور دولة المؤسسات. ويظل يحدث هذا في بلادنا — رغم

وجود شواهد تؤكد الوعي المبكر بخطر الــزعيم الفرد — وكما قال نابليون بونابرت، في مطلــع القرن التاسع عشر: **"الرجال عاجزون عن ضمان المستقبل، وحدها المؤسســات تحــدد مصائر الأمم."**

ومع صعود القائد **"الكاريزما"** يتـــوارى الاقتصاديون المتخصصون، ويحل محلهم مــبررون ومادحون ورافعو شعارات، فيها عموم وعاطفية أكثر مما فيها من العلمية والاســتجابة للمنطــق والعقل، وتصبح أنشطة اقتصادية معينة مقدســة لمجرد أنها من شارات الهوية الوطنية، وكأن التغيير يحمل خيانة ضمنية للأجداد، ومن المؤكد أن علينا إجلال أجدادنا، لكــن دون تخريــب مســتقبل أحفادنا.

وغالباً يترافق صعود القائد الكاريزما مع

نوع من المغالاة. وفي تجربتنا عجزت نخبة التحرر الوطني عن التمييز بين "**دولة قاسية**" و"**دولــة قوية**". فالدولة العنيفة ليست دولة قويــة، لأنهـا تعتمد بشكل رئيس على أدوات إكراهية وإدارية لتخترق المجتمع، أما الدولة القوية فتعتمد الليونــة والإقناع، فتظهر قدرة على التغـيير للأفضــل، بالتعاون مع مراكز القوة في المجتمع بدلاً من الهيمنة عليها.

والسلطة الاستبدادية، المحررة من القيــود القانونية، تتيح للدولة التصرف على نحو اعتباطي وتمنح انطباعاً بالقدرة الكلية، وسرعان ما يتبــدد هذا الانطباع بظهور ثغرات التطبيق. هذه الدولة تستخدم الرمزية والمجازية لمساعدتها في الحكــم، لكن نادراً ما تسعى للشرعية عبر حســن الأداء. وقدرة دولة ما على جمع الضرائب المباشرة، بدلاً

من غير المباشرة، مؤشر موثوق عن قوتها الفعلية وقبول الشعب لشرعيتها على أساس الأداء. ويجب ألا تؤخذ ادعاءات الاستبداد في تعجيل عملية التطور بقيمتها الظاهرية.

ومعظم أصحاب القرار وكثير مثقفينا في أذهانهم خريطة لا تميز بين **"السلطة"** و**"القـوة"**، فالسلطة تعني امتلاك قوة غير مكتوبة، كما تعـني التأثير الجاذب للسلوك المثالي لتلقـي الاحتـرام والطاعة وهي تترافق على نحو قاطع مع النفـوذ، لكن ليس بالضرورة مع القوة، بمعنى القدرة على إجبار آخرين على فعل ما لم يكونوا ليفعلوه لولا الإكراه. وللتمييز بين السلطة والقوة أهمية كبيرة، لأنه اعتراف بأن الدولة لا تملك مخزوناً لا ينضب من القوة الإكراهية، بشكل يسمح لها بالاعتمـاد عليه باستمرار، بل يجب أن تسـتخدم السـلطة

الإكراهية باقتصاد، وأن تعتمد بشكل رئيس على سلطتها لتكسب إجماعاً حول سياساقا لتـأمين التجاوب الطوعي.

فمفهوم الدولة القوية المشار إليه عفا عليه الزمن، ومع ازدياد الاهتمام العالمي بحقوق الإنسان والمجتمع المدني أصبحت قوة الدولة "**داخليـــاً**" لا تقاس بقدرقا القمعية بل قدرقا على بلورة تراض يوازن بين الحرية والأمن. ومن النتائج الخطـيرة المترتبة على الانحياز لخيار "**السيطرة**" على المجتمع، تسييس دور الأجهزة الأمن، وهـــذا الاسـتدعاء للأمن لساحة السياسة كما أنه يـــؤدي لتحـــول الفعل السياسي من الجدل والتنافس للصدام فإنـــه في الوقت نفسه يؤدي لنتيجة أخرى هي الأخطر، إذ تتحول هذه الأجهزة لصانع قـــرار، وعندئـــذ تصبح الرصاصة والهرواة سـيد الموقـف، ومـــع

تضخم نفوذها فإن الأجهزة وبشكل — شبه تــام — تصبح "حزباً سياسياً". وبدخول أجهزة الأمن ساحة السياسة من الباب تخرج الديموقراطية مـــن "الشباك". !

الأمنية والنبوءة والتصور المستقبلي

قد لا يكون من الـــدقيق أو الموضـــوعي الحديث عن "**العقل العربي**" وإطـــلاق الأحكـــام عليه، لكن من المؤكد أن الموضوعية لا تتعارض أبداً مع الإقرار بحقيقة أن تياراً فكرياً يغلب عليـــه الانتماء اليساري (الماركسي والقـــومي) يقـــود الثقافة العربية منذ أكثر حـــوالي ستين عامـــاً، وبالتحديد منذ خرجنا من "**حفـــرة**" الاستعمار لنهوي في بئر الاستبداد، ونسأل الله ألا يكـــون "**بئراً بلا قرار**"!

هذا العقل يعاني ─ ضمن مـــا يعـــاني ─ الوقوع في أسر الماضي في رؤيته للذات والعـــالم معاً، وعندما وضع ابن خلـــدون أســـس علـــم الاجتماع وضع ─ دون أن يدري ─ أسس "**علم**

المستقبليات"، فمحاولة تجريد قواعــد للعمـران البشري كانت تعني بالضرورة اضطراد بعضهـا بشكل شبه ثابت، ومع الوصول لمثل هذه القوانين يصبح التوقع والاستشراف متاحاً.

وبقدر ما تعد السياســة مواءمــة بــين متعارضات ومفاوضة بين خصوم يعد "**التخطيط السياسي**" للمستقبل مسعى للتحكم في عوامل لو تركت دون تدخل فإنها تتفاعل بحرية، وهنا نجــد سبيكة من: إدراك واقعي وخيال محسوب وطموح لاستباق الآتي.

والمستقبل مساحة عريضة من الإمكـان تتحول بالبصيرة الثاقبة لمخطط يمكن إنجازه مهما بدا كبيراً. واتخاذ الواقع مبــدأ ومنتهـى للنظــر السياسي يفضي للجمود والتحول من "**فاعل**" إلى "**منفعل**" وفي كل رؤية كونية، "**محددات**" رؤيــة

مستقبلية يمكن البناء عليها، لكن العقل السياسي العربي أصيب بعجز عن التخيل، ومن يراجع مثلاً تجارب النجاح الاقتصادي الشرق آسيوية في نصف القرن الماضي ويقارنها بحصيلة الفترة نفسها من مسيرتنا يذهله البون الشاسع بين "**قـدراتنا**" و"**قدرنا**". فمثلاً، تجارب النمور الآسيوية لم تكن لتنجح لولا خيال سياسي جرئ. وهذه السمة توجد غالباً في الأمم ذات الثقافات الغنية عندما يحكمها الخوف بأن ذاتها مهددة، فعندئذ تصبح كل خطوة محل شك وموضع تردد.

ولنأخذ مثال انهيار الاتحاد السوفيتي، فقد كان بالنسبة للأمريكيين: أمنيةً ونبوءةً وتصوراً مستقبلياً، فمنحتهم الأمنية أملاً، وأعطتهم النبوءة ثقة، وكان التصور المستقبلي جسراً بين الكـائن والمأمول. وخلال التاريخ الغربي طرحت تصورات

لمستقبل العالم، صحيح أن كثيراً منها بدأ وانتهى بجرد **"تصورات"**، لكن تحول المستقبليات من التنجيم إلى **"علم"** ضيق الهوة كثيراً بين الكلام عن المستقبل وتخطيطه.

وعندما يكون لدى صانع القرار العربي ملف عنوانه: **"هكذا نريد العالم"**، نكون قد بدأنا طريقنا لبناء المستقبل، لا عبر التمني وبناء الأسوار العالية لتحمينا من السيناريوهات المستقبلية للآخرين، بل بوضع سقف يناسب طموح أمة تملك مقومات تمكنها من المساهمة في صياغة مستقبل العالم. والمستقبل الذي لا نجتهد لتخيله وتخطيطه هو في الغالب مجهول سوف يدهمنا ونحن غافلون. والتفكير في الحاضر والتخطيط للمستقبل لا يكادان ينفصلان، وكم من حاضر أهدر المستقبل أو وأده قبل ميلاده.

ومن التوازن الغائب يمتد التنــاقض بــين أدبيات التمني والبكائيات الحارة على حالنــا، إن "**أدبيات التمني**" في ثقافتنا مزدهرة أيما ازدهــار وينافسها في الازدهار بكائيات مريرة على حالنا، وبين النقيضين المتطرفين نعاني فقــراً في الأفكــار رغم أن القرنين الماضيين كانا العصــر الــذهبي للأفكار ودورها في التــاريخ، بــل إن الأفكــار أزاحت — وإلى الأبد — دور عوامل مثل: القوة، والإرادة، والموارد الطبيعية، والثقل الســكاني، في تحديد شكل المستقبل.

وما نقصده بغياب الأفكار غياب الأفكار الكبيرة المحركة للتاريخ، فالفكرتــان الكبيرتــان خلال القرنين التاسع عشر والعشرين (الرأسماليــة والاشتراكية) نشأتا في الغرب، والأمر نفسه ينطبق على الأفكار الكبيرة في: الإدارة والقانون الدولي

والتنظيم التكنولوجي، بل لم تشهد ثقافتنا أفكاراً مهمة في الفكر العسكري، فرغم الصعود المشهود لروح العسكرة في بلادنا، لم يظهر لدينا مفكر يمكن إدراجه في طابور صناع تاريخ الفكر العسكري، من الصيني صن تزو إلى الألماني كلاوزفيتز.

ومن أسباب غياب الأفكار الكبيرة في عالمنا التغييب المتعمد لـ **"صناع الأفكار"**، وفي اليابان تحت الحكم الفاشي كانت علاقة السياسيين وأصحاب الفكر علاقة عداء فتمتع السياسيون بالسلطة ومزاياها وظل مستواهم الثقافي متدنيا. وكانت كراهية المفكرين للسلطة — مضافة لافتقارهم للاستقلال المالي — سببا لمنعهم من المشاركة السياسية فأصبح دورهم محدوداً، وبلغ ضعفهم حد تلقيبهم بألقاب منها:

"المفكرون الضعفاء"، "المتملقون الأذلاء"، ولذا لم يستطيعوا كبح جماح العسكريين اليابانيين، حتى وصلت اليابان للكارثة.

ومن أسباب غياب الأفكار الكبيرة أيضاً، الخلط بين "القيم" و"الأفكار"، فما أرساه الإسلام من قيم ومعايير في الاجتماع الإنساني جعل البعض يعتقد أن إعمالها وحده يصنع النهضة، ما جعل معظم المثقفين لا يشغلون أنفسهم أساساً بالأفكار، وهذه القيم كانت محل احترام عندما نقل الخليفة عمر بن الخطاب فكرة الدواوين مثلاً، وهي الفكرة التي كانت منعطفاً تاريخياً، فالإجابات التي قدمها الإسلام هي في مجال المعايير والأهداف، وليس الوسائل.

فإذا انتقلنا للواقع العربي، وجدنا مؤسسات تعليم تحولت إلى "مدارس عليا" تخرج

الآلاف من المتعلمين المفتقرين لصفات الشخصية الابتكارية الفعالة العاجزين عن التفكير النقدي، وهي خطيئة سببها قناعتنا بأن كل الأجوبة محددة سلفا وعلينا العمل وسيحدث التقدم آلياً.

ومع غياب الشروط الموضوعية لازدهار دور الأفكار في الواقع غابت مصانع الأفكار كجزء من تحييد المجتمع المدني كله: الأحزاب، الجمعيات، الأوقاف، وتقليم أظافره بشكل قاسٍ، كثمرة لمناخ شمولي عم بلادنا مع نشوء الدولة الوطنية، والآن ــ بعد نصف قرن ــ فإن من خرجوا من دمار الحرب العالمية الثانية، وكان شاملاً، ربحوا المنافسة مـــع أمـــم، خرجـــت في التوقيت نفسه تقريبا مـــن آثار الاستعمار، والرابحون كانوا مسلـــحين بـــ "**الأفكـــار**"، والخاسرون كانوا مسلحين بـ "**الإرادة**".

والمشكلة أعمق بكثير من المفاضلة بـــين الأفكار المطروحة على الساحة والأوزان النســبية لأتباعها، أو حتى وجاهة مقولاتها، إذ يستشـــعر المواطن العربي أن المشكلة مشكلة جدوى، فمـــا معنى أن أقيم الأفكار المطروحة لأختار لافتة أقف تحتها، إذا لم يترتب على الاختيار حق أصحابه في الدعوة لأفكارهم ومنافسة الآخرين في مضـــمار محدد وفق قوانين توضع لتحترم؟

فكيف نتصور أن تتقدم أمتنا وشـــعوبها محرومة من حقها في الديموقراطية كتداول للسلطة، والقضاء النزيه المستقل كميـــزان لعلاقـــة كـــل الأشخاص الطبيعــــيين والاعتبـــاريين، والحريــــة الاقتصادية كمناخ تنافس اقتصادي شفاف، والحق في المعرفة والمساءلة، كشـــبكة متكاملـــة مـــن التشريعات والممارسات تمكن المواطن الفرد مـــن

الحصول على المعلومات، والحق في مساءلة الحاكم والرقابة على أعمال الحكومة؟ إن العزوف عـــن المشاركة في الحاضر، والزهد في الحلم بمســـتقبل أفضل، ليس نجاحا لأجهزة الأمـــن السياســـي في تحقيق "الاستقرار"، بل جرس إنذار، والمجتمعات تصاب بـــ "السكتة السياسية" قبل أن تنفجر أو تموت!

وهم الصراع بين الوطنية والديموقراطية

ليس من التشاؤم القول بأننا خرجنا مــن صراع القوى في القرن العشرين وقــد تحطمــت قوانا، فمفهوم القوة السائد عربياً لا يعني إلا القوة العسكرية، وللمفارقة لم يؤد هذا لضمان الأمــن العربي المحاصر بتهديدات عديدة. لكننا خرجنا من العصر الذهبي للأفكار بوهم، ترسخ حتى صــار ييدو علامة مميزة، هو أن بلادنا تشهد صراعاً بين الوطنية والديموقراطية. أما الأفكار الــتي لاكتــها ألسنة المثقفين وأقلامهم عقوداً، فظلــت بجــرد مقولات لم تختبر في معتركات حقيقية تساعد على بلورتها، ولذا فليس غريباً ألا توجــد اشــتراكية عربية، أو ليبرالية عربيــة، فهــي في وجودهــا

النخبوي مجرد ترجمة عربية لأفكار غربية، كأنها مقتنيات متحف فكري مفتوح!

وتحت هذه المظلة هناك خلط بين: الهوية والأيديولوجيا والسياسة، فالهوية محصلة تفاعل طويل بين عوامل كثيرة (دينية – ثقافية – اجتماعية – اقتصادية – لغوية) وهي متغيرة تطالها التحولات، وإجاباتها هي بالأساس عن أسئلة ثقافية. أما الأيديولوجيا فتكاد تكون نقيض السياسة، فالسياسة مفاوضة ومواءمة ولا تقبل الأيديولوجيا، ذلك أن الأيديولوجيا تبدأ من امتلاك القول الفصل المطلق، وهي نقطة تنتهي عندها السياسة!

ولنعد للوراء قليلاً، فمنذ قرنين تقريباً، وقضية النهوض هم عربي لا يتوقف المثقفون العرب عن الاجتهاد لتحديد سياقاته وممكناته،

وبعد قرنين لم نزل ندرس الإشــكاليات، بينمــا تجارب النهوض، شرقاً وغرباً، تتوالى في مجتمعات لا تملك ما نمتلكه من قدرات ماديــة ومعنويــة وبعضها عانى قسوة عامل خارجي يبلغ أضــعاف ما عانيناه. ومن يتأمل الــ "**وصفات**" المطروحــة للعلاج يجد قوائم سوداء تحدد ما يجب هدمه، أما ما يجب بناؤه فلا يكاد يعرفه أحد، فهناك دعوات لمواجهة الاستعمار، واستغلال رأس المال، والقضاء على الرجعية، وكأن النهوض إذا قمنــا بــذلك سيأتي حتماً، لأنه قدر عربي قادم لا محالة، لا يمنعه إلا هذه الحواجز.

ولأننا لا نكاد نجد تصوراً نظرياً متكاملاً لمشروع نهوض عربي، فإن محاولاتنا المجهضة تخضع للتقييم في ضوء دور العامل الخارجي أو كفــاءة التنفيذ وحسب، أما مرتكزات الرؤية فلا نكــاد

نقيمها. بل إن أحداً لا يستطيع تبرير حتمية ارتباط العروبة بالاشتراكية، كما لو كان اقترافهما قدراً، رغم أن الرأسمالية قبل المد العروبي كانت موجودة تحقق بنجاحات مشهودة، واعتبارها "**ثمرة محرمة**" لا يبرره ماضي الاستعمار في بلادنا. والأمر نفسه ينطبق على الارتباط غير المبرر بين القومية والاستبداد وبالتالي الموقف العدائي الذي تتخذه الثقافة القومية من الديموقراطية، وبخاصة أن بلادنا شهدت قبل موجة الانقلابات العسكرية القومية تجارب ديموقراطية، ما يعني أن الاستبداد لم يكن حتمياً.

وقد أصبح صدور التقارير التنموية الدولية مناسبة سنوية لنشعر بالحرج، والدرس الأهم فيها يتجاوز الأرقام والإحصاءات إلى ضرورة الاعتراف بفشلنا، كشرط موضوعي للبحث عن

بداية جديدة.. ..بداية لا نخلط فيها بين الهوية والأيديولوجيا، وفيها أيضاً لا تصادر النخب حقوق الناس في الاختيار والإبداع. وفي الوقت نفسه تكون بداية لا تهدر فيها تجارب الآخرين الناجحة في التنظيم السياسي والاجتماعي، بسبب مواقفهم من قضايانا التي لا شك في عدالتها.

ومما يجب الاعتراف به أن أحوالنا — مع استثناءات قليلة — تتراجع في: الاقتصاد والتعليم والحريات، وكأن بلادنا تغرق ببطء، وتتجه لمصير مظلم، بينما دعوات الإصلاح محاصرة بالشكوك والاتهامات، ومساعي التغيير مكبلة بأفكار وخيارات يريدها البعض **"مقدسة"**، ويعتبر التخلي عنها خروجا عن الوطنية وتخليا عن الهوية، رغم أنها في النهاية مجرد **"خيارات"** يجوز العدول عنها.

ومن لم يتعلم من دروس التاريخ فإنما

يتجاهل أميز ما فضل الله به الإنسان، وهو أنـــه كائن "**ذو تاريخ**"، وبالتالي قادر على التعلم مـــن خبرات السابقين، ومن أراد رؤية عاقبة السير ضد التاريخ فلينظر إلينا!

ومن الحقائق الثابتة في الاجتماع الإنساني أن بين البشر على اختلاف هوياقم مشترك هـــو الفطرة، ولكن الصعود الكبير للعروبة بجاوز دوره في تعزيز الإحساس بـــالاختلاف عـــن الآخـــر "**المستعمر**"، ليصبح شرنقة تفصلنا عن العالم، حتى أصبحنا نختصر رؤيتنا لعلاقتنـــا بالعــــالم بعبـــارة واحدة: "**إحنا حاجة تانية**"!

ودروس إعادة البناء بعد الحروب كـــثيرة وبعضها صادم، ومن حقائق التجربة اليابانية أنـــه بنهاية الحرب تحولت أكثر من مئة مدينة إلى رماد، وأعاد اليابانيون بناء ما دمرته الحـــرب في ثلاثـــة

أعوام!

فهل حالنا أسوأ من حالة اليابــان بعــد الحرب العالمية الثانية؟

إن عبرة ذلك أن إعادة إعمار ما دمرتــه الحرب أيسر كثيراً من إعادة بنــاء مــا دمــره الاستبداد، فنحن مثقلون ومقيدون بمنطق تفكــير نخبتنا أكثر مما نحن محاصرين بمؤامرات الأعــداء، ولا تنقصنا الفرصة، ولا الموارد، ولكن تنقصــنا الشجاعة. وللأسف، فإن كــثيرا مــن مثقفينــا خائفون من "**الشارع**"، وهذا يــدفعهم أحيانــاً لإخفاء قناعاتهم ورفــع شــعارات جماهيريــة، لاسترضاء الرأي العام، وبسبب ذلــك، يــزداد بشكل ملحوظ تعامل العقل العربي مع القضــايا بتضاؤل ملحوظ للتحليل العقلاني، لتحــل محلــه مواقف تدغدغ المشــاعر وتســتدر صــيحات

الإعجاب، فالمزاج الجماهيري لا يحتمل ترف التحليل، وهو ما تعبر عنه بصدق القصة الساخرة الشهيرة عن طبيب يستدعى لمريض ميئوس من شفائه فيعتبر نطقه بالتشخيص سببا في قتل المريض! وعليه، فإن أطباء التحليل السياسي العربي يفر كل منهم **"فراره من الأسد"**، من ورطة أن يكون هو من يعلن الحقيقة. ومزاج الجماهير مزاج مواجهة وحشد لا يعرف المواءمة، وبالتالي، فإن كل حديث عن حلول وسط يعد خيانة وعمالة و... ..!!!

وعندما يصبح الخطاب السياسي مقيداً بالزعيم، ومكمماً بالجماهير، فليس أمامه مساحة ليقول شيئاً مفيداً أو جديداً. وعندئذ تصبح كل بضاعته إعادة إنتاج خطاب القائد ترديداً وتأكيداً. وإذا عاد إلى الماضي، كانت عودته

انتقائية، تختار ما يخدم القناعة المحددة مسبقاً، وكأننا أمام عملية علاج نفسي تتعامل مع الوجدان وخيالاته، لا مع العقل والمنطق وحقائقه. ومن يمسكون دفة توجيه الجماهير يستطيعون في هذا المناخ خنق الرأي المخالف، وهو مشهد يشبه المشهد السوفييتي قبل جورباتشوف، حيث خنقت دعوات المراجعة، لكن الجماهير هنا حلت محل اللجنة المركزية للحزب الشيوعي وأجهزة الأمن السياسي، فأصبحت الجماهير عبئاً على من حشدوها، وأصبح المثقف "**جرسوناً**" (نادلاً) يقدم لسيده ما يريده، بعد أن كان رائداً يستدل به الناس. والويل لأمة تقودها الجماهير.

وفي النهاية:

فإن سيطرة هذا الخليط من الأفكار على العقل العربي هو نبع الموجات المتلاحقة من

"**أعراس الدم**"، فإذا لم نضع نهاية لهذه الأعراس..

..وإذا لم ننجح في فض الاشتباك الموهـــوم بـــين الوطنية والديموقراطية، فسوف يكـــون الغـــرق مصيرنا جميعاً: حكامـــاً ومحكـــومين، مـــثقفين وجماهير، والعلاج الوحيد هو "**الديموقراطية**".

حتى لو أقسم البعض بأغلظ الأيمان علـــى أنه "**مر!**".